COBBLESTONE® · THE CIVIL WAR

Stonewall Jackson

Spirit of the South

Cobblestone Publishing
A Division of Carus Publishing
Peterborough, NH
www.cobblestonepub.com

Staff

Editorial Director: Lou Waryncia
Editor: Meg Chorlian
Book Design: David Nelson, www.dnelsondesign.com
Proofreaders: Meg Chorlian, Sarah Elder Hale, Eileen Terrill

Text Credits

The content of this volume is derived from articles that first appeared in *COBBLESTONE* magazine. Contributors: Mary Price Coulling, Gina DeAngelis, Louise K. Dooley, Margie J. Harding, Marta Kastner, Michael Anne Lynn, Jerry Miller, Marian Harrison Novak, James I. Robertson, Jr., and Sylvia Whitman.

Picture Credits

Courtesy Virginia Military Institute Museum, Lexington, Virginia: 3; Library of Congress: 4, 5, 9, 10, 11, 12, 13, 16, 22, 23, 26, 30, 31, 32-33, 36, 37, 38, 40; courtesy Virginia Military Institute Archives, Lexington, Virginia: 7; courtesy Stonewall Jackson Foundation, Lexington, Virginia: 18; Fred Carlson: 14-15, 44-45; The Library of Virginia: 41. Images for "Civil War Time Line," pages 44-45, courtesy Photos.com, Clipart.com, and Library of Congress.

Cover

Jackson Entering Winchester
Valentine Richmond History Center

Library of Congress Cataloging-in-Publication Data
for *Stonewall Jackson: Spirit of the South* is available at http://catalog.loc.gov.

Printed in China

Cobblestone Publishing
30 Grove Street, Suite C
Peterborough, NH 03458
www.cobblestonepub.com

Table of Contents

An Ambitious Lad 4

An Air of Determination 7

Bravery Under Fire......................................9

Map: The War Between the States.............14

Life in Lexington 16

The Famous Nickname 20

An Important Mission:
The Shenandoah Valley Campaign 22

Jackson Makes His Move: Second Manassas 26

Chancellorsville:
A Cunning Win and a Stunning Loss 31

Little Sorrel 38

Major Jackson and Cadet Walker 41

Words to Live By.......................................43

Civil War Time Line 44

Glossary...46

Index 47

Surrounding this portrait of Thomas J. "Stonewall" Jackson is his boyhood home in present-day West Virginia.

An Ambitious Lad

Thomas (Tom) Jonathan Jackson spent most of his childhood getting shuffled from one extended family member to another. Born on January 21, 1824, in Clarksburg, Virginia (now West Virginia), he was preceded by an older sister, Elizabeth, and an older brother, Warren. Tom's mother, Julia Neale Jackson, was well educated, attractive, and lively. His father, Jonathan Jackson, was a lawyer but a poor businessman who had lost properties that his father had given him, and the family had fallen into debt.

Tragedy Strikes

When Tom was two years old, Elizabeth caught typhoid fever. Julia was expecting another child, so Jonathan took over the nursing duties. Elizabeth died on March 6, 1826. Jonathan, who also had contracted the disease, died three weeks later, on March 26. Tom's younger sister, Laura, was born the next day.

Julia tried to keep the family together by sewing and running a school, but she found it difficult to make ends meet. On November 30, 1830, she married Blake B. Woodson, an older lawyer and widower with eight children, none of whom lived under his roof. Warren was sent to live with his mother's relatives. The following year, while Julia was pregnant with her fifth child, her health began to decline. Tom and Laura also were sent away to live with relatives. Shortly after giving birth to another son in the fall of 1831, Julia died.

Searching for a Home

Tom and Laura were living then with their father's family at Jackson's Mill near Weston, Virginia (now West Virginia). It was a bustling place presided over by his step-grandmother and uncle Cummins Jackson. All sorts of cousins, uncles, and aunts lived nearby. Tom liked it there, describing it as a place where he was "surrounded by my playmates and relatives, all apparently eager to promote my happiness."

When Tom was 11, his step-grandmother died. He was sent to live with another relative, his uncle Isaac Brake, while his sister went to live with their mother's family. Tom did not like living with Uncle Brake. He soon ran away and appeared hungry and wet at another

Jackson's Mill, where young Tom lived with his Uncle Cummins, was an idyllic setting for a country boy.

relative's house. His explanation was to the point: "Uncle Brake and I can't agree. I have quit [him]." The family let Tom return to Uncle Cummins's.

A Big Adventure

Tom's biggest adventure took place in 1836, when he was 12 years old. He and his 16-year-old brother, Warren, traveled to the Ohio River to visit their sister, Laura. Laura was living with their uncle Alfred Neale, who sold wood to steamboats. Warren and Tom

decided to try to support themselves by selling firewood to passing boats. They traveled down the Ohio River, crossed the border into Kentucky, and eventually arrived on the Mississippi River. They returned to the Neales' around February 1837, thin and threadbare. All they had to show for their adventure were two new trunks. After that, Tom went back to live with Uncle Cummins.

Steamboats needed plenty of firewood to cruise up and down the Mississippi River, allowing men such as Jackson's uncle, Alfred Neale, to make a living by supplying wood.

During these years, Tom's schooling was limited to classes taught by traveling teachers. Altogether, he had only a few years of formal education. At best he learned to read, write, and do some arithmetic. Years later he said, "When I was young I committed the blunder of learning to read before I learned to spell well." Despite this, Tom taught school for four months when he was 16. He had five students and was paid $5.64 for his work. He also worked as a constable of Lewis County, Virginia (now West Virginia), serving legal papers on people and collecting bad debts.

But Tom was an ambitious lad — he knew that he needed an education if he wanted to make something of himself. So in 1842, when he had an opportunity to apply for admission to the U.S. Military Academy in West Point, New York, he took it. He was accepted and began his military education and career that year.

An Air of Determination

Dressed in homespun clothing and carrying all his possessions in two old saddlebags, 18-year-old Thomas J. Jackson arrived in West Point, New York, in June 1842. He looked like what he was — an awkward country boy. But he had an air of determination about him. One classmate commented, "That fellow looks as if he has come to stay."

Hard Work

Staying was not easy. Although Jackson was ready for military life, he lacked the required social graces and found it difficult to make friends. He also was not prepared for the rigorous academic schedule. Whereas many other cadets had come from preparatory schools or colleges, Jackson could not even do fractions and decimals. And he was not a quick study; he had to work very hard to catch up.

People remembered Cadet Jackson as an earnest young man who spent most of his time studying. At night he piled his heating grate with coal and studied in its light as long as it lasted. His greatest challenge came in the first year. He had only a provisional appointment and had to pass a difficult exam in order to continue at the academy. During the mathematics exam, he wrote with such fierce determination at the blackboard, trying to solve his problem, that even his fellow students were impressed.

One of his teachers later wrote that Jackson "was not what is now termed brilliant, but he was one of those untiring matter-of-fact persons who never would give up an undertaking until he

This likeness of Jackson — a copy from a daguerreotype — was done in Mexico City in 1847. It captures the somber determination for which Jackson was known at West Point.

accomplished his object. He learned slowly, but what he got in his head he never forgot."

A Bad Joke

Although Jackson never became popular with his classmates, he won their respect. One time another cadet substituted his dirty musket for Jackson's clean one before an inspection. The cadet probably thought it a joke, but for Jackson it was a serious matter. He was able to identify his musket by a secret mark, and he demanded an investigation. Other cadets tried to talk him out of it, but he insisted that it was a matter of honor. Jackson felt that the other cadet had lied and should be punished, even if it meant his expulsion from the academy. It took a lot of persuasion before Jackson agreed not to pursue the matter.

Jackson's first two years at West Point were the hardest. He feared that he would fail and be sent home. In addition to mathematics, Jackson had a hard time with French, having never studied it before. By the end of his second year, however, his grades had improved, although he still had trouble with drawing. "I could never do anything in that line to satisfy myself or anyone else," he noted.

Jackson had been last on the list of the 92 students who had qualified for the academy in the examinations of 1842. When he graduated in 1846, he was 17th in a class of 59. His hard work and determination had paid off.

Cadets were expected to keep their rifles clean — a responsibility Jackson took very seriously.

Bravery Under Fire

While Thomas J. Jackson had studied warfare at the U.S. Military Academy, he learned what war was really like in Mexico. Jackson was 22 years old when the U.S.–Mexican War (1846–1848) offered him the opportunity to demonstrate his bravery as a soldier.

The Battle of Churubusco was one of the last battles leading up to the U.S. capture of Mexico City. Mexico's defeat led to the addition of California, New Mexico, and the territory that would become Nevada, Utah, Colorado, and Arizona to the United States.

Increasing Tensions

Boundary disputes resulting from the annexation of Texas in 1845 sparked a war between the United States and Mexico. President James K. Polk and his supporters wanted to expand U.S. territory into the sparsely settled western lands of the United States. The newly established Mexican government claimed the same lands.

Parts of this land previously had been controlled by colonial Spain, which had also governed Mexico until it gained its freedom in 1821.

The U.S.–Mexican War increased tensions in the United States between the North and the South by raising the question of whether slavery should be permitted in the new territories. It also served as an important training ground for many of the officers who later fought on both sides in the Civil War, including Jackson, Robert E. Lee, Ulysses S. Grant, and Barnard E. Bee (who was credited with giving Jackson his famous nickname during the Battle of First Manassas in 1861).

Jackson received his commission in the U.S. Army in 1846, right before he graduated from West Point. After a short furlough to visit his family, Jackson joined Company K, 1st Regiment of Artillery, under Captain Francis Taylor in New York. The regiment traveled south to New Orleans, Louisiana, then on to Mexico. Taylor's troops reached Monterrey, Mexico, in late November, after General Zachary Taylor's troops had taken the city in fierce fighting. Jackson

Jackson got his first experience of actual warfare in Mexico at places such as Cerro Gordo.

An Interest in Religion

As a boy in rural western Virginia, Thomas J. Jackson was exposed to religion, but his church attendance was probably irregular. Jackson's interest in religion grew during the U.S.–Mexican War. His commanding officer, Captain Francis Taylor, was a deeply religious man who shared his views with the men under his command. Daily encounters with death may have made Jackson and other soldiers think more about spiritual matters.

Shortly after Jackson returned to the United States, he was baptized in an Episcopal church in New York. He continued to explore religious issues. When he moved to Lexington, Virginia, in 1851, he became acquainted with Reverend William White, minister of the Lexington Presbyterian Church. He came to regard Reverend White as his commanding officer in matters of religion.

Jackson soon became a devout member of the Lexington Presbyterian Church. He taught Sunday school, served as a deacon, and established a Sunday school for African Americans, both slaves and free blacks. He tithed and strictly observed the Sabbath, refraining even from traveling on Sunday.

Religion became increasingly important to Jackson. His strong faith helped him to deal with the deaths of his first wife and child and later the death of his second child. It also was a source of confidence and support for him during the Civil War.

The Battle of Veracruz began with an amphibious assault on the city and ended after a 20-day siege.

was disappointed to have missed the early fighting. He commented to a new acquaintance, "I really envy you men who have been in action. We who have just arrived look upon you as veterans. I should like to be in one battle."

In the Thick of It

In January 1847, Captain Taylor's forces joined those under General Winfield Scott at Port Isabel, on the Gulf of Mexico, for an amphibious assault on Veracruz. Jackson won a commendation for "gallant and meritorious conduct" at Veracruz and was promoted to brevet first lieutenant. During the army's march inland to Mexico City, Jackson participated in the Battle of Cerro Gordo and was promoted again for bravery under fire at Contreras, Churubusco, and Chapultepec. Between his graduation in June 1846 and September 1847, Jackson was promoted an impressive three times.

As an officer in an artillery unit, Jackson was one of a highly trained group using the latest developments in military science. He belonged to a company of light, horse-drawn artillery that was frequently called "flying artillery." During the Battle of Contreras, when the commander of a battery was mortally wounded, Jackson took his place. Jackson's commanding officer later praised him for his leadership.

Jackson Holds His Ground

Jackson's finest moment in Mexico was at the castle of Chapultepec, a fortification built on a high hill with steep sides, which made attacking it difficult. While other troops surrounded the hill and scaled the wall with ladders, artillery batteries (including Jackson's) were ordered to advance down a narrow road below the hill, toward Mexico City.

The approach was blocked by Mexican artillery and a deep ditch. Jackson's battery came under heavy fire from the front and from above. Many men and horses were killed, and many soldiers retreated, but Jackson held his ground. He and a sergeant moved an artillery piece into position and continued to attack with only one gun. The men rallied and soon succeeded in destroying the Mexican battery.

U.S. troops surrounded and took the palace, then moved on to Mexico City. Jackson was among a small group that pushed far ahead of the infantry along the causeways to the gates of the city, which fell on September 14, 1847.

Jackson earned a number of commendations from his superior officers for his service during the U.S.–Mexican War. Following his famous role at the storming of Chapultepec, he was promoted to brevet major.

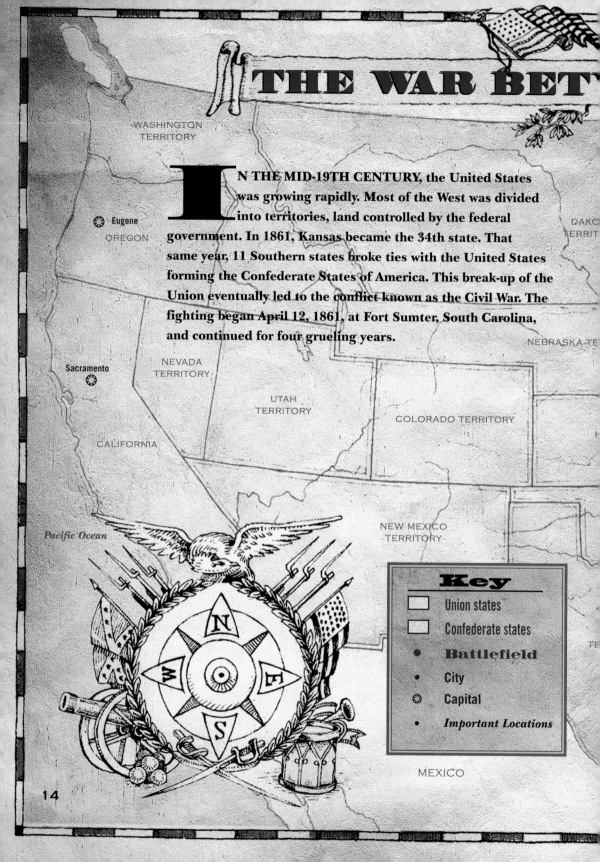

WASHINGTON TERRITORY

IN THE MID-19TH CENTURY, the United States was growing rapidly. Most of the West was divided into territories, land controlled by the federal government. In 1861, Kansas became the 34th state. That same year, 11 Southern states broke ties with the United States forming the Confederate States of America. This break-up of the Union eventually led to the conflict known as the Civil War. The fighting began April 12, 1861, at Fort Sumter, South Carolina, and continued for four grueling years.

Eugene
OREGON

DAKO
TERRIT

NEVADA
TERRITORY

Sacramento

NEBRASKA-TE

UTAH
TERRITORY

COLORADO TERRITORY

CALIFORNIA

Pacific Ocean

NEW MEXICO
TERRITORY

Key

☐ Union states

☐ Confederate states

● **Battlefield**

● City

✸ Capital

● *Important Locations*

MEXICO

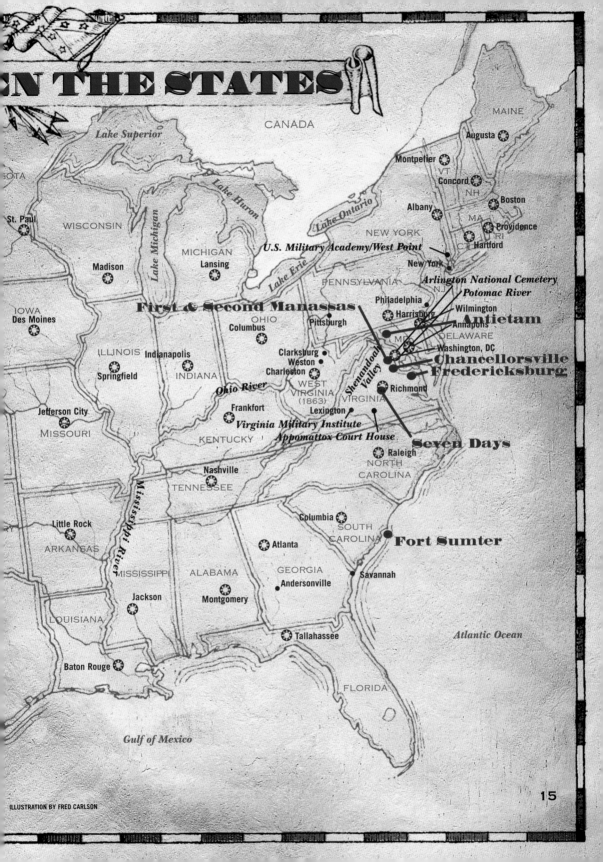

CANADA

Lake Superior

MAINE

Augusta ✿

Montpelier ✿

Lake Huron

VT

Concord ✿

NH

Boston ✿

St. Paul ✿

WISCONSIN

Lake Michigan

Albany ✿

MA

Providence ✿

RI

MICHIGAN

Lansing ✿

Lake Ontario

NEW YORK

Hartford ✿

Madison ✿

Lake Erie

U.S. Military Academy/West Point

CT

New York ✿

IOWA

Des Moines ✿

PENNSYLVANIA

NJ

Arlington National Cemetery

Potomac River

First & Second Manassas

OHIO

Columbus ✿

Pittsburgh ✿

Philadelphia ✿

Harrisburg ✿

Wilmington

DELAWARE

Antietam

ILLINOIS

Indianapolis ✿

Clarksburg ✿

Weston ✿

Charleston ✿

MD

Annapolis ✿

Washington, DC

Chancellorsville

Springfield ✿

INDIANA

WEST VIRGINIA (1863)

Ohio River

Shenandoah Valley

Richmond ✿

Fredericksburg

Jefferson City ✿

Frankfort ✿

Lexington ✿

VIRGINIA

MISSOURI

Virginia Military Institute

Appomattox Court House

KENTUCKY

Raleigh ✿

Seven Days

Little Rock ✿

Nashville ✿

TENNESSEE

NORTH CAROLINA

ARKANSAS

Columbia ✿

SOUTH CAROLINA

Mississippi River

Atlanta ✿

Fort Sumter

MISSISSIPPI

ALABAMA

GEORGIA

Savannah ✿

Jackson ✿

Andersonville ✿

Montgomery ✿

Atlantic Ocean

LOUISIANA

Tallahassee ✿

Baton Rouge ✿

FLORIDA

Gulf of Mexico

ILLUSTRATION BY FRED CARLSON

After the U.S.–Mexican War, Jackson taught at the Virginia Military Institute in Lexington. Today, a statue of Jackson stands in front of the cadet barracks where he once lived with his students.

Life in Lexington

A new professor of natural and experimental philosophy and instructor of artillery tactics arrived at the Virginia Military Institute (VMI) in August 1851. The professor, Major Thomas J. Jackson, was 27 years old and very uncomfortable in the classroom. However, with the determination and faith he exhibited throughout his life, he believed firmly that because God had led him to this teaching assignment, he would succeed. "I knew that what I willed to do, I could do," he said. The institute and its surrounding village — Lexington, Virginia — would offer Jackson a place to call home.

Success and Failure in the Classroom

Jackson found teaching artillery tactics relatively easy. After all, he had graduated from the U.S. Military Academy at West Point and had served as an artillery officer in the U.S.–Mexican War. Before long, the young men under his supervision became skilled at calculating distances and choosing projectiles, such as bullets and cannonballs, as well as loading and firing the institute's brass guns and howitzers.

Teaching the basics of physics (optics, acoustics, and analytical mechanics) was far more difficult. Each evening, Jackson memorized his lesson for the next day, a lecture he delivered in a dull monotone. If a cadet answered a question in a way that varied even slightly from the text, Jackson reprimanded him for being incorrect. Students who complained that they did not fully understand material were given verbatim oral repetitions of Jackson's lectures.

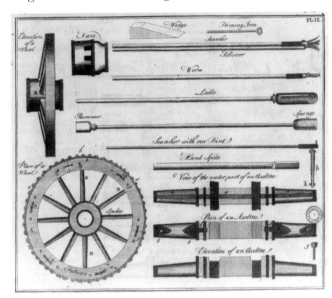

Not surprisingly, "Old Jack," or "Tom Fool Jackson," as he was sometimes called, was not popular with his students, and he quickly became the butt of jokes and pranks. Cadets laughed at his rigid military bearing, his large feet, his strict adherence to rules, and his awkwardness in setting up laboratory experiments. But the most conscientious among them recognized the man's sincerity and his willingness to admit even the slightest mistake. For example, Jackson once roused a sleepy cadet from bed so that he could correct a misinterpretation he had made in class.

Sticking to Routine

During his first two years at VMI, Jackson's living quarters were in the cadet barracks. After his marriage to Elinor Junkin in 1853, they lived with her parents on the nearby Washington College campus. It was not until 1858, after he married a second time, that Jackson purchased the only home he ever owned, a few blocks from

Fast Fact
Washington College was renamed Washington and Lee University in 1871. Robert E. Lee, Jackson's commanding officer during the Civil War, served as the college president from 1865 to 1870.

Elinor and Mary Anna

Thomas J. Jackson was a bachelor when he arrived in Lexington to teach at the Virginia Military Institute. He soon fell deeply in love with Elinor (also spelled Eleanor) Junkin, the attractive, witty daughter of a Presbyterian minister and president of Washington College, which was located next to the institute. Jackson and Ellie were married in August 1853.

When Ellie died in October 1854 after giving birth to a stillborn baby boy, Jackson was devastated.

Three years later, he married Mary Anna Morrison of North Carolina, whose father also was a Presbyterian minister and former college president. The couple's first child, Mary Graham, was born in 1858. She lived only a few months. Their second daughter, Julia, was born in November 1862, during the Civil War. Jackson saw Julia only twice — once when Mary Anna and Julia visited him near Fredericksburg, Virginia, in April 1863, and again on his deathbed the following month.

For more than 50 years after Jackson's death, Mary Anna Jackson — a small, dignified woman who always dressed in black — was the South's best-known widow and a public symbol of the suffering and loss of many Confederate women. She died in 1915 and today lies buried with her two daughters and her husband beneath the Stonewall Jackson Monument in the Stonewall Jackson Cemetery in Lexington.

VMI. Here he maintained his unwavering daily schedule: an early-morning cold bath in both winter and summer, a brisk walk, family prayers, breakfast, classroom teaching at the institute, midday dinner at home, hours quietly working in his garden. Every evening, standing before his high desk, he memorized his lecture for the following morning.

To many of Lexington's citizens and certainly to VMI cadets, Jackson seemed a stern, humorless man. But within the privacy of his home, he was far more relaxed. He laughed, danced, and played pranks on his wife. Jackson also became an important citizen of the small college-centered community. He was part owner of a tannery and served on the board of a local bank. He joined one of Lexington's literary debate societies and was an active member of the Presbyterian Church.

Gardening's Rewards

Jackson also bought some farmland on the outskirts of town and became the owner of six slaves. In the afternoons, when Jackson was not teaching at the institute, he worked with his slaves in the garden behind his house or on his farmland at the edge of town. Gardening was Jackson's favorite recreation.

In the mid-19th century, the ability to grow fresh fruits and vegetables largely determined the quality and variety of a family's

Gardening was a popular 1800s pastime, and a particular favorite recreation of Jackson.

diet. Jackson, who was known to be "as methodical as a multiplication table," was systematic in his gardening and cultivated his crops in quite a scientific way. He followed a planting calendar prepared for him by a fellow officer, and he depended on Robert Buist's popular gardening guide, *The Family Kitchen Gardener*. His copy of the book, which is at the Virginia Historical Society, has the word "plant" written beside certain items and pencil marks beside the sections on asparagus, watermelon, mustard, onions, parsley, parsnips, spinach, tomatoes, turnips, sorrel, apples, apricots, cherries, currants, gooseberries, grapes, nectarines, peaches, pears, plums, and quince.

Jackson's 10 years in Lexington ended abruptly in the spring of 1861, when he was ordered to march VMI's Corps of Cadets to Richmond, Virginia, at the beginning of the Civil War. He did not live to see again the village he loved so well.

Fast Fact

Jackson suffered from dyspepsia, a digestive ailment. He believed that a person's health could be improved by drinking and bathing in fresh mineral water.

Jackson's actions at the Battle of First Manassas helped to ensure a Confederate victory and earned him one of the most famous nicknames in military history.

The Famous Nickname

When the Civil War began with the Confederate attack on Union-held Fort Sumter, South Carolina, on April 12, 1861, both the North and the South believed the war would be short and decisive. Each side hoped to take the other's capital — Washington, D.C., in the North and Richmond, Virginia, in the South. With only about 100 miles between these two cities, northern Virginia became the place where both the North and the South focused their armies. Within three months, they clashed in northeastern Virginia in the first major land engagement of the war. The battle became known as Manassas in the South for the nearby railroad junction and Bull Run in the North for the stream around which the battle was fought.

A Clash of Armies

In July 1861, a hastily organized Union force led by General Irvin McDowell moved from Washington, D.C., 30 miles into northern Virginia. Its goal was the vital railroad junction at Manassas. Learning of their movements, the Confederates just as hastily marshaled a force to protect the junction. The Southerners took a battle position along the banks of a stream called Bull Run.

> "Look! There stands Jackson like a stone wall!"
> — Barnard E. Bee

The opposing sides were new to the ways of war. Thousands of untried recruits and unpolished armies collided in the rolling countryside. Throughout the morning that hot July 21, the Federals sought to break the Confederate left flank. The Southern soldiers, however, showed their determination to hold their line. The key to the area was Henry House Hill. Brigadier General Thomas J. Jackson and a brigade of 3,500 Virginians went into line behind the crest of the hill and out of sight of the assaulting Federals. Jackson's orders were to hold the hilltop at all costs.

Early in the afternoon, Union troops broke through the Confederate frontlines and swept up Henry House Hill in anticipation of victory. Jackson's five regiments were all that stood between them and success. The Southern commander calmly ordered his men forward to the crest of the hill.

The Famous Cry

General Barnard E. Bee, whose Confederate lines had been shattered in the heavy fighting earlier in the day, saw the new position. Bee galloped among his retreating soldiers, supposedly shouting, "Look! There stands Jackson like a stone wall! Let us determine to die here, and we will conquer!" It remains unclear whether Bee meant the cry as a criticism of Jackson because he simply stood there and did not enter the fight, or if Bee wanted to point out how strong Jackson looked and meant it as a rallying cry.

Either way, Jackson's men did stop the Union attack, opening the way for a Southern victory later that day. Bee was mortally wounded in the final action, never knowing that his battle cry had produced one of the most famous nicknames in American military history.

Fast Fact

Officially known as the 1st Brigade, the "Stonewall Brigade" was the only Confederate brigade permitted to have its nickname become its official army designation.

21

Though the Shenandoah Valley looks very peaceful in this view from the Maryland Heights, control of the valley was important to the strategy of both armies during the Civil War.

An Important Mission

The Shenandoah Valley Campaign

Tucked between the Blue Ridge Mountains and the easternmost ranges of the Allegheny Mountains is the Shenandoah Valley, or the Valley of Virginia, as it is often called. The corridor stretches 165 miles from Lexington, Virginia, to the Potomac River.

Fast Fact

The Shenandoah Valley offered a safe retreat route for the Confederate army after Antietam (September 1862) and Gettysburg (July 1863).

Control Is Key

Running in a southwest-to-northeast direction, the valley was like a spear pointing at the heart of the North during the Civil War. An invading Confederate army could drive straight through it toward targets such as Harrisburg, Pennsylvania. However, if an invading Union army followed the valley south, it would be marching away from the North's principal goal: the southern capital of Richmond, which lay to the east. Yet a Union force moving due south through Virginia had to control the Shenandoah Valley to protect its western flank.

Aside from its strategic importance, the valley was a rich source of wheat, corn, fruit, and livestock. Known as the "Breadbasket of the Confederacy," it supplied the South's leading army — the Army of Northern Virginia — with food. Throughout the Civil War, the residents of the valley supported the Southern effort.

Confederate major general Thomas J. "Stonewall" Jackson was in command of the region early in 1862. With a pathetically small force of 3,500 soldiers, Jackson was charged with protecting the Shenandoah Valley from Union invasion and blocking Federal forces in that area and in Fredericksburg, to the east, from moving to assist Union general George B. McClellan in his grand offensive against Richmond. Jackson was well aware of the importance of his mission. "If this Valley is lost," he told a friend, "Virginia is lost."

A Bold Move

In March, Jackson learned that Union troops were leaving the northern end of the valley and marching east to aid McClellan. On March 23, Jackson attacked at Kernstown, just south of Winchester. The superior number of Union forces repelled Jackson's assaults, but the engagement was a strategic victory for the South because Jackson's boldness forced a stop to the Federal withdrawal from the valley. Instead of moving toward Richmond, Union troops began converging on the valley from three different directions.

Jackson won a series of victories, including a battle at Cross Keys, that forced the Union army to withdraw from the Shenandoah Valley.

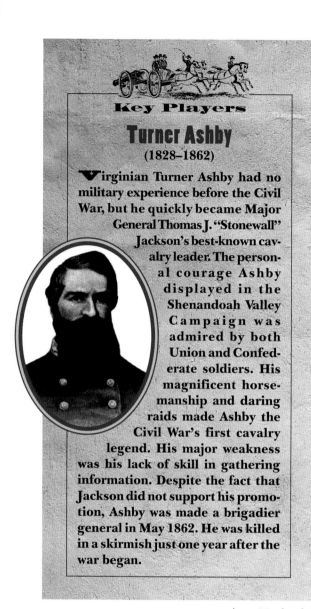
Having fallen back to the southern end of the great corridor, Jackson repulsed the advance of one enemy force in a late-afternoon fight at McDowell on May 8. The Confederate general secured reinforcements that increased his numbers to 17,000 men. He then swept through the valley, overwhelmed a Federal garrison at Front Royal on May 23, and two days later overran a Union force at Winchester. Union soldiers fled for safety across the Potomac River.

"Old Jack," as his men affectionately called him, then withdrew southward. Two enemy armies gave pursuit, and just as they were about to unite, Jackson struck hard. On June 8, he defeated one Union force at Cross Keys. After a sharp battle the following day at Port Republic, he sent the other army into retreat. The Shenandoah Valley was now clear of Union invaders.

Singlehanded Success

In 40 days of marching, Jackson had led his men more than 400 miles over difficult terrain ranging from mud to mountains. He had fought six engagements plus a dozen delaying actions. Total Union casualties were at least 5,400 men; Confederate losses were but half that number. Jackson's men captured 10,000 small arms; 500,000 rounds of ammunition; a dozen cannon; wagonloads of equipment; tons of foodstuffs such as bacon, hardtack, and coffee; and more medical supplies than may have existed in the entire Confederacy at the time.

Jackson's success was due in large part to his knowledge of the terrain, singleness of purpose, and self-confidence gained from

The Shenandoah Valley Campaign earned Jackson the respect and awe of friends and enemies alike.

the firm belief that his troops were "an army of the living God." He also drove his troops hard, kept his plans secret, and attacked unexpectedly, often delivering a heavy blow at a strategic point.

By the end of the Shenandoah Valley Campaign, not only had Jackson repelled every Union strike against him, but he also had defeated forces outnumbering him three to one. His campaign, a Northern officer said, "ended in the complete derangement of the Union plans in Virginia." Although Jackson was little known in March 1862, by the summer of that year he had become the most famous soldier of the war.

A year after the two armies first clashed at Manassas, Jackson and Major General James Longstreet led the Confederate army to a second victory at the same site.

Jackson Makes His Move

Second Manassas

From his headquarters at Bristoe Station, Virginia, Union major general John Pope saw an orange glow in the sky on the night of August 27, 1862. The bright light told him that Confederate major general Thomas J. "Stonewall" Jackson's troops were burning the Union supply base five miles away at Manassas Junction. But Pope was delighted to have found the sly Jackson, so he issued an order for his army to converge on Manassas: "If you will march promptly and rapidly, we shall bag the whole crowd."

Fight at Brawner's Farm

Unfortunately for Pope, though, Jackson had no intention of staying there. Instead, he deployed his men into the woods north of Groveton, a tiny hamlet west of the Manassas battlefield of 1861. On August 28, 1862, as Federal troops marched toward Centreville on the Warrenton Turnpike, Jackson's army attacked Union brigadier general Rufus King's division at John Brawner's farm west of Groveton.

The fighting at Brawner Farm was the fiercest in the war to date: One of every three men was shot. King's troops, some of them green, suffered heavy losses, but they managed to hold off Jackson's army until evening and then withdrew to Manassas.

Meanwhile, that same day, Confederate generals Robert E. Lee and James Longstreet, along with 25,000 men, approached Manassas from the west. Pope, in his eagerness to "bag" Jackson and concentrating all his efforts on this, did not leave enough troops to stop these Rebel reinforcements at a pass through the Bull Run Mountains called Thoroughfare Gap.

Piecemeal Approach

On August 29, Pope ordered an attack on Jackson's line. Jackson's men had hidden behind the embankments formed by an unfinished railroad bed

Key Players
Robert E. Lee
(1807–1870)

Like Thomas J. Jackson, Robert E. Lee graduated from the U.S. Military Academy at West Point and served in the U.S.–Mexican War. A native of Virginia, Lee resigned from the U.S. Army when his native state seceded from the Union. By June 1862, Lee was in command of the Army of Northern Virginia, and Jackson's commanding officer. In several key battles — the Shenandoah Valley Campaign, Second Manassas, and Chancellorsville — Lee split the forces under his command, each time sending Jackson to divert or distract the enemy. In victory and defeat, for three years Lee kept the Confederate army intact and ready to fight another day, despite having fewer men and supplies. In the final year of the war, Union general Ulysses S. Grant pursued Lee relentlessly until the great Southern commander was forced to surrender at Appomottax Court House, Virginia, on April 9, 1865. Lee encouraged his fellow Southerners to make peace and work to unite the country, and many historians consider him the greatest military commander of the Civil War.

James Longstreet
(1821–1904)

While one wing of General Robert E. Lee's Army of Northern Virginia was led by Major General Thomas J. "Stonewall" Jackson, the other wing was commanded by General James Longstreet. Like Lee and Jackson, Longstreet's pre-Civil War military history included attendance at West Point and fighting in the U.S.–Mexican War. Longstreet fought in most of the major engagements that included Lee's Army of Northern Virginia. He was wounded in the Wilderness Campaign of 1864. Although at times he lacked decisiveness when working independently, Longstreet proved an able commander and a devastating force when following Lee's battle plans. Lee affectionately referred to him as "My Old War Horse."

north and northeast of Groveton. About 32,000 Union soldiers faced Jackson's 22,000 Confederates. But instead of sending a large corps all at once, Pope had small brigades advance one after another. Despite this piecemeal approach, Union troops actually broke Jackson's line on several occasions. Each time, however, Federal reinforcements arrived too late, giving the battered Confederates a chance to regroup. Jackson and his men repulsed every attack, holding their position until Lee and Longstreet could get there.

Vague Orders

Also that day, Pope gave vague orders to Union major general Fitz John Porter to advance west of the battlefield. But Porter unexpectedly faced a Confederate unit much larger than his own: It was Longstreet's wing of the Army of Northern Virginia, the other half to Jackson's wing, recently arrived from Thoroughfare Gap.

Despite having given unclear orders, Pope convinced himself that Porter would attack Jackson's right. This proved impossible, however: Pope did not realize that Longstreet had deployed on Jackson's right. Pope felt that Porter — a friend of former Union major general George B. McClellan — purposely was refusing to advance. When Pope's second — and this time, more direct — order reached Porter after 6 P.M., it was too late to attack.

That night, Pope saw that the worn-out Rebels on Jackson's left had pulled back. Pope incorrectly believed that Jackson was retreating, but Jackson had merely ordered his men back to an

earlier line. Pope ordered Porter to move his fresh troops the next morning into position to pursue Jackson.

Throwing Rocks

When Porter began to move on August 30, instead of ambushing retreating Confederates, his troops faced a heavily defended battle line. Pushing forward anyway, the Union soldiers encountered rapid and deadly fire as they drew closer to the entrenched Confederates.

It was a scene of intense and close fighting. Jackson's exhausted men, who were out of ammunition, actually threw rocks at the Northern soldiers! And some Union men threw them right back. At the end of the day, Jackson's troops held their ground, but Jackson finally asked Longstreet to send help.

When Porter had moved his troops that morning to "pursue" Jackson, he had left the field in front of Longstreet clear for an attack. Before reinforcing Jackson, however, Longstreet first sent an artillery unit that devastated the Federal attackers. Realizing now the Union army's left was weakened, Lee ordered Longstreet to launch his own massive attack.

A Smashing Victory

Pope had not prepared for this. Union troops were either slaughtered or swept from the field as Longstreet's men pushed

Strengthened by Longstreet's reinforcements, Jackson and his men forced the Union army to retreat toward Washington, D.C.

Because of vague orders from Major General John Pope, Major General Fitz John Porter (pictured here with his staff) walked into a situation where his odds of beating Jackson were very slim.

their line eastward. Finally, that evening, Pope understood he was beaten and hurried to protect his line of retreat. Thanks to some quick-thinking officers and the hard-fighting Union soldiers on Chinn Ridge and Henry Hill, Pope's defeated army made an orderly retreat and was not destroyed, as Lee had hoped.

On August 31, the Union army held strong positions in Centreville. To avoid being cut off by Lee, however, Pope continued to withdraw his men back to Washington, D.C., on September 1. Instead of trapping Jackson, Pope had fought an unnecessary battle on the ground of Jackson's choosing. Nearly 20,000 men were killed or wounded — about 10,000 Federals and more than 9,000 Rebels. For the Confederacy, Second Manassas was a smashing victory.

Second Manassas also made Lee recognize the formidable fighting force he commanded in the combination of Longstreet and Jackson. As he did at Second Manassas (and earlier, in June, at Seven Days), Lee would turn to Jackson and Longstreet twice more in 1862 as he tried to capture the Union army between these two well-led wings of the Army of Northern Virginia: at Antietam in September, and at Fredericksburg in December.

Chancellorsville

A Cunning Win
and a Stunning Loss

Under cover of
darkness, fellow
Confederates mistook
Jackson and his
comrades for Union
soldiers. This artist's
rendition shows a
wounded Jackson on
the Chancellorsville
battlefield.

Too busy fighting in Virginia to attend the birth of
his daughter, Julia, in November 1862, Thomas J.
"Stonewall" Jackson nevertheless longed to see
her. In April 1863 he asked his wife, Mary Anna, to bring the five-
month-old baby from North Carolina. Jackson moved out of his

31

The Battle of Chancellorsville was a brilliant victory for Confederate general Robert E. Lee, whose bold choices helped him defeat a much larger army.

army tent and into a nearby house, where he arranged for Julia's baptism and showed her off to friends and staff. News that Union troops were crossing the Rappahannock River near Fredericksburg abruptly ended the family visit. After nine days as a proud father, Jackson returned to war.

Devising a Plan

Union brigadier general Joseph Hooker was moving to cut off the Confederate forces from Richmond. Hooker had twice as many soldiers as Robert E. Lee, but Lee had Jackson. Together, they devised a daring plan.

Northern troops were gathering near Chancellorsville, a crossroads in a messy forest known as the Wilderness. But Hooker had failed to protect the right side of his army. If the Confederates could sneak past that flank, they could sandwich Hooker's men between two Southern forces.

Jackson, who was coming down with a cold, stayed up late studying maps with Lee before falling asleep by the campfire. At dawn, staffers brought the news the generals wanted to hear: There was a road leading to Hooker's rear.

Spotted!

Lee decided to remain in front of the Union line with 14,000 troops, pretending to represent the whole Army of Northern Virginia. Meanwhile, Jackson was to race 28,000 men and more than 100 heavy guns around Hooker's weak side.

Jackson's regiments marched out early on May 2. They had strict orders not to talk or cheer. The weather was perfect — sunny and clear. Rain had left the ground damp, preventing dust clouds from rising from the soldiers' feet.

Nonetheless, Union troops spotted Jackson's column on an exposed hill. Jackson rerouted his equipment to a back road but

Fast Fact

The Union army suffered more than

17,000

casualties at Chancellorsville. The Confederate army casualties were nearly

13,000.

After Jackson was shot, four soldiers hurried to carry him on a stretcher to the nearest field hospital.

ordered his men to press on. As reports trickled back to Union officers, they assumed the Confederates were retreating. Jackson caught a glimpse of a Federal camp. Unsuspecting soldiers were playing cards and harmonicas while cooks prepared a meal.

A Surprise Attack

Late in the afternoon, the Confederates lined up in the Wilderness. After marching more than a dozen miles, they were hungry and tired, but excited. Jackson gave the go-ahead. Bugles sounded, and the Confederates yelled as they charged forward. Stunned, Union troops watched birds spring from the forest, followed by deer, rabbits, foxes, squirrels — and the enemy. Hooker's men panicked and ran, chased by the Southerners, some of whom paused to spear hunks of beef from abandoned plates with their bayonets.

The surprise attack succeeded. As darkness fell, Jackson rode out to gather information and see where the Union army had gone. In the confusion after the charge, Confederate soldiers were regrouping in the Wilderness. Hearing horses, the 18th North Carolina opened fire. Officers ordered them to stop, but Major John Barry mistook his fellow Southerners for Union soldiers. He yelled, "It's a lie! Pour it into them, boys!" They did not realize it was Jackson returning from his reconnaissance.

Three Bullets

Three bullets hit Jackson, one lodging in his right palm and two breaking bones in his left arm. Officers helped the general off his horse, Little Sorrel. They hurriedly called for a doctor; Union troops were roaming the woods. Jackson's staff rounded up a stretcher and four soldiers to carry it. One was shot, but someone took his place. Another tripped on a vine, sending Jackson crashing to the ground on his shattered arm. Finally, after a bumpy ambulance ride, the general arrived at a field hospital. The surgeons all agreed that they had to amputate the left arm to save his life.

Lee ordered Jackson moved to a house far from enemy lines. "Tell him to make haste and get well, and come back to me as soon

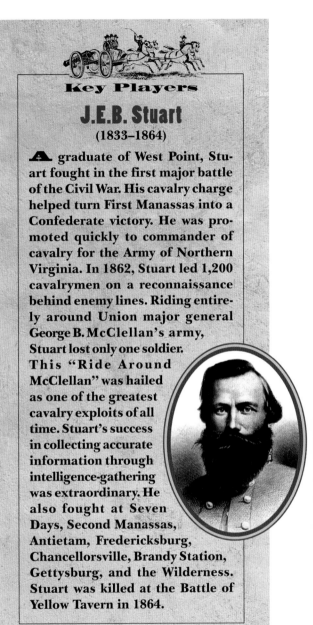

Key Players

J.E.B. Stuart
(1833–1864)

A graduate of West Point, Stuart fought in the first major battle of the Civil War. His cavalry charge helped turn First Manassas into a Confederate victory. He was promoted quickly to commander of cavalry for the Army of Northern Virginia. In 1862, Stuart led 1,200 cavalrymen on a reconnaissance behind enemy lines. Riding entirely around Union major general George B. McClellan's army, Stuart lost only one soldier. This "Ride Around McClellan" was hailed as one of the greatest cavalry exploits of all time. Stuart's success in collecting accurate information through intelligence-gathering was extraordinary. He also fought at Seven Days, Second Manassas, Antietam, Fredericksburg, Chancellorsville, Brandy Station, Gettysburg, and the Wilderness. Stuart was killed at the Battle of Yellow Tavern in 1864.

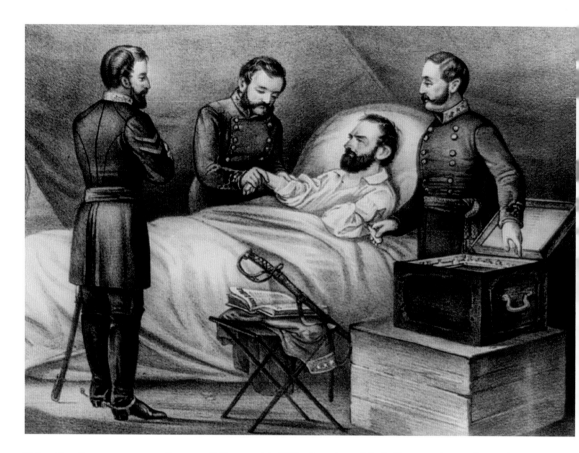

as he can," Lee said. "He has lost his left arm; but I have lost my right arm."

Last Words

Over the next few days, a mysterious pain in Jackson's side developed into pneumonia. When Mary Anna and Julia arrived on May 7, he was feverish and losing consciousness. On Sunday, May 10, doctors told Mary Anna that her husband would die that day. She talked to him about God's will and asked where he wanted to be buried. Then she brought Julia, smiling, to his bedside.

Jackson refused a drink of brandy because he wanted to remain clear-headed. In the afternoon, his mind returned to the battlefield. "Let us cross over the river, and rest under the shade of the trees," he said. Then he died.

The Confederacy mourned a hero. After a stop at the capitol in Richmond, Jackson's coffin traveled by train and canal boat to

Lexington. There his body was laid out overnight in his old classroom at the Virginia Military Institute, guarded by cadets. After a funeral at the Presbyterian church, Jackson was buried beside his daughter Mary

> ## "He has lost his left arm; but I have lost my right arm."
> ### — Robert E. Lee

Graham in the church cemetery. In 1891, Jackson's remains and those of his two daughters were moved to the crypt beneath the Stonewall Jackson Monument in Lexington, Virginia.

To General Robert E. Lee, Jackson's death meant the loss of a daring and irreplaceable officer.

The triumph of Chancellorsville and the tragedy of the accidental shooting added to Jackson's glory. One newspaper wrote, "He occupied a place in the heart of every friend of his country." After the Civil War, defeated Southerners raised money dime by dime to memorialize their leaders. Today, visitors to Lexington find above the Jackson family crypt a granite monument topped by a bronze statue. Unveiled in 1891, it portrays Jackson surveying the battlefield, one hand on his sword, the other holding field glasses.

In most Civil War portraits of Jackson on horseback, he appears to be a gallant rider on a graceful warhorse. In reality, Jackson rode a gentle mount and seemed awkward in the saddle.

Little Sorrel

Everyone knows that a general's warhorse is supposed to be a handsome, spirited animal. It is supposed to charge into battle, terrifying the enemy with a ferocious glare.

But Major General Thomas J. "Stonewall" Jackson's mount,

Little Sorrel, did not fit that description at all. He was short and plump, had soft brown eyes, and would rather jog than gallop. Fortunately, his smooth gait and quiet disposition made Little Sorrel the ideal horse for Jackson, who was a great general but often had the appearance of an awkward rider.

Easy to Handle

Jackson acquired his favorite mount when a number of Federal horses were captured by Confederate forces at Harpers Ferry, Virginia (now West Virginia), in 1861. Jackson's officers chose two sorrel horses, a small one — Little Sorrel — to send to his wife, Mary Anna, and a larger one — Big Sorrel — for the general. Jackson, however, preferred the smaller mount because he was easy to handle.

Little Sorrel was about 11 years old, plain brown with no white markings, and rather chunky. Standing only 15 hands high (60 inches at the top of his shoulder), he looked too small for Jackson. Yet the sturdy beast carried his master easily for great distances, sometimes covering 40 miles a day.

Horse and rider were hardly an inspiring sight — Jackson, in his worn uniform, slouched on the plodding horse — but Confederate soldiers cheered the pair whenever they appeared. Embarrassed by these displays, Jackson would spur Little Sorrel into a canter to escape the scene as soon as possible. Before long, Little Sorrel learned to gallop away whenever cheering began.

A Steady Friend

The horse had a gentle personality. He was a placid, agreeable mount who was rarely excited about anything except food. He was so quiet that his master could, and often did, fall asleep while riding. Little Sorrel himself preferred to lie down during rest breaks, sometimes stretching flat out on the ground.

In the midst of battle, Little Sorrel was usually not gun-shy or nervous. He did not require much attention, so Jackson could concentrate on his battle plans and how they were carried out rather than care for his horse. Jackson rode Little Sorrel in most of his battles during the Shenandoah Valley Campaign.

Fast Fact

On July 20, 1997,

111

years after the animal's death, Little Sorrel's remains were laid to rest in a grave on the Virginia Military Institute's grounds.

Little Sorrel was a faithful and good-tempered horse, memorialized here with his famous master in Washington, D.C.

A Popular Attraction

Jackson was on Little Sorrel on May 2, 1863, when Confederate forces mistook him for an enemy scout and fired on him in the final stages of the Battle of Chancellorsville. After Jackson's death and funeral, Little Sorrel was sent to Mary Anna Jackson at her family's farm in North Carolina. When the war was over, he made regular appearances at Confederate reunions and fairs, where he was a popular attraction among war veterans, who remembered Jackson with great affection.

For several years, Little Sorrel lived at the Virginia Military Institute. An old horse, he was treated as an honored guest. He spent his last days as a beloved pet at a home for Confederate veterans in Richmond, Virginia. After his death in 1886, Little Sorrel's hide was carefully mounted over a plaster mold. Today it stands in an exhibit on Jackson at the Virginia Military Institute Museum.

Major Jackson and Cadet Walker

Their paths first crossed in 1851, when James Alexander Walker was a 19-year-old first classman (fourth-year cadet) at the Virginia Military Institute (VMI) and 27-year-old Major Thomas J. Jackson was VMI's newly appointed professor of natural and experimental philosophy and instructor of artillery tactics. Though dedicated and hard-working, Jackson was not a success in the classroom, and students — Walker among them — made him the object of practical jokes and ridicule.

In his later years, James Alexander Walker was proud of his association with Jackson and worked to honor the general's memory.

Clashing Personalities

Walker was popular, self-assured, and bright. He was especially talented in physics, a class Jackson taught. In the spring of 1852, the struggling but strict professor criticized the method the boy had used to calculate the time of day by the angle of the sun. Walker objected. The argument grew heated, and Jackson ordered Walker to sit down and be silent. Instead of following institute regulations requiring a cadet to obey a professor's direct order, Walker refused. Jackson put him under arrest.

In the court-martial that followed, Walker defended himself vigorously. Nevertheless, he was found guilty of disobedience of and disrespect toward a superior officer and dismissed from the institute. His anger and disappointment were apparently deep, for it is said that he threatened Jackson. After Walker's dismissal, the superintendent of VMI wrote to the cadet's father, "I would advise you to come up at once and take [your son] home, as I have reason to believe he may involve himself in serious difficulty." The expulsion, only weeks before graduation, was a bitter blow to the proud youth.

Meeting Again

Walker, resolving to succeed elsewhere, earned a law degree from the University of Virginia in 1855 and practiced that profession until April 1861, when Virginia entered the Civil War. Walker became captain of the Pulaski Guards, a company he raised and trained, and was assigned to Jackson's brigade. When the brigade first saw action in early July, its men performed gallantly, particularly Walker. When told to report to Jackson, Walker was apprehensive, for he now knew how wrong he had been that spring of 1852. He had come to understand that "duty" and "obedience" were "necessary principles of life."

He found Jackson sitting in front of his tent. Walker, expecting a rebuke, stood "erect, [with] his head thrown back," but Jackson "extended his hand and greeted Walker in a most friendly way."

> "If Stonewall Jackson was not a hero, then the history of the world…never knew a man worthy to wear that title."
> — **James Alexander Walker**

'Stonewall Jim'

Walker soon became a lieutenant colonel. He and his regiment followed Jackson to victory at First Manassas in July 1861. As colonel of another regiment, Walker fought under Jackson at Fredericksburg in December 1862, then followed Jackson to Chancellorsville in May 1863.

As Jackson lay dying from complications from wounds he received at Chancellorsville, he was told that the leader of his old brigade, General E.F. Paxton, had been killed. It is not known whether Jackson named Paxton's successor, but soon after Jackson's death, Walker was given the brigade, by then called the Stonewall Brigade. Walker led it honorably until it was disbanded, making him its last commander and earning him the nickname "Stonewall Jim."

After the war, Walker continued to honor his former professor and general. One of his proudest official acts was to serve as chief marshal at the 1891 unveiling of Jackson's statue in Lexington, Virginia. "If Stonewall Jackson was not a hero," he once said, "then the history of the world…never knew a man worthy to wear that title."

Words to Live By

While at West Point, Thomas J. Jackson kept a book of maxims, or sayings, which he wrote down in a notebook. Later, he also began to record quotations from letters or speeches that had impressed him. He was determined to improve his character and better himself, and he returned to the notes he had made and the sayings he had collected throughout his life. Etiquette books and self-improvement literature were popular during Jackson's time, providing him with good sources of material. Principles and rules of conduct such as "Disregard public opinion when it interferes with your duty" guided him throughout his life.

Following are some of the mottoes by which Jackson, according to his second wife, Mary Anna, "shaped his own conduct and character":

"Through life let your principal object be the discharge of duty."

"Sacrifice your life rather than your word."

"Resolve to perform what you ought; perform without fail what you resolve."

"A man is known by the company he keeps."

Following are some sayings associated with the Civil War:

"People who are anxious to bring war don't know what they are bargaining for; they don't see all the horrors that must accompany such an event."

"We will give them the bayonet."

"My duty is to obey orders."

"When you charge, yell like furies!"

"I trust that God will grant us a great victory."

CIVIL WAR

1860

Lincoln

NOV 6
Abraham Lincoln is elected 16th president of the United States.

1861

Davis

FEB 9
Formation of the Confederate States of America (CSA) by secessionist states South Carolina, Mississippi, Florida, Alabama, Georgia, Louisiana, and Texas. Jefferson Davis elected CSA president.

MAR 4
Lincoln's inauguration

APR 12

Fort Sumter (South Carolina)
Civil War begins with Confederate attack under Gen. Pierre Beauregard.

APR 15
Lincoln issues proclamation calling

for 75,000 troops. Gen. Winfield Scott becomes commander of Union army.

APR 17
Virginia joins CSA, followed by Arkansas, Tennessee, and North Carolina.

APR 20
Gen. Robert E. Lee resigns from U.S. Army and accepts command in Confederate army.

JUL 21
First Manassas (Virginia)
Gen. Thomas J. "Stonewall" Jackson defeats Gen. Irvin McDowell.

NOV 1
Gen. George B. McClellan assumes command of Union forces.

1862

FEB 11-16
Fort Donelson (Tennessee)
Gen. Ulysses S. Grant breaks major Confederate stronghold.

MAR
McClellan begins Peninsular Campaign, heading to Richmond,

Virginia, the Confederate capital.

APR 6-7
Shiloh (Tennessee)
Grant defeats Beauregard and Gen. A.S. Johnston. Heavy losses on both sides.

APR 24

New Orleans (Louisiana)
Gen. David Farragut leads 17 Union gunboats up Mississippi River and takes New Orleans, the South's most important seaport.

JUN 25-JUL 1
Seven Days (Virginia)
Six major battles are fought over seven days near Richmond, Virginia. Lee is victorious, protecting the Confederate capital from Union occupation.

Halleck

JUL 18
Lincoln turns over command to Gen. Henry W. Halleck.

AUG 29-30
Second Manassas (Virginia)
Jackson and Gen. James Longstreet defeat Gen. John Pope.

SEP 17
Antietam (Maryland)
McClellan narrowly defeats Lee. Bloodiest day in American military history: 23,000 casualties.

SEP 22

Lincoln issues preliminary Emancipation Proclamation, freeing slaves in Confederate states.

OCT 3-4
Corinth (Mississippi)
Gen. William Rosecrans defeats Gen. Earl Van Dorn.

NOTE: Battles are in black type, with flags indicating: Union victory Confederate victory

TIME LINE

NOV 7
Lincoln replaces McClellan with Gen. Ambrose Burnside to lead Army of the Potomac.

Burnside

DEC 13
Fredericksburg (Virginia) Lee defeats Burnside.

1863

JAN 1
Final Emancipation Proclamation frees slaves in Confederate states. Union army begins enlisting black soldiers.

JAN 25
Lincoln replaces Burnside with Gen. Joseph Hooker.

Hooker

JAN 29
Grant is placed in command of the Union army in the West.

MAY 1-4
Chancellorsville (Virginia) Lee defeats Hooker.

JUN 28
Lincoln replaces Hooker with Gen. George E. Meade.

JUL 1-3

Gettysburg (Pennsylvania) Meade defeats Lee.

JUL 4
Vicksburg (Mississippi) After weeks of seige, Grant takes the Confederate stronghold on Mississippi River, effectively dividing eastern and western Confederate forces.

SEP 18-20
Chickamauga (Georgia) Gen. Braxton Bragg defeats Rosecrans.

OCT 16
Lincoln puts Grant in charge of all western operations.

NOV 19
Lincoln delivers the Gettysburg Address, dedicating the battlefield as a national cemetery.

NOV 23-25
Chattanooga (Tennessee) Grant defeats Bragg.

1864

MAR 9
Lincoln puts Grant in command of entire Union army. Gen. William T. Sherman takes over western operations.

MAY 8-21
Spotsylvania (Virginia) Grant defeats Lee.

MAY 31-JUN 12
Cold Harbor (Virginia) Lee defeats Grant and Meade.

JUN 15-18

Petersburg (Virginia) Lee and Beauregard defeat Grant and Meade.

NOV 8
Lincoln is re-elected.

NOV 15-DEC 21
Sherman's "March to the Sea." Sherman destroys supplies and transportation systems from Atlanta to Savannah (Georgia), crippling the Confederacy.

Lee

1865

APR 2
Petersburg (Virginia) Grant defeats Lee. Confederates leave Richmond.

APR 9
Lee surrenders to Grant at Appomattox Court House, Virginia.

APR 14
Lincoln is shot by John Wilkes Booth at Ford's Theatre, Washington, D.C. He dies the following morning.

DEC 6
Thirteenth Amendment to the Constitution abolishing slavery is ratified.

GRAPHICS BY FRED CARLSON

45

Glossary

Ammunition: Anything that can be thrown or shot — such as a bullet, rock, or cannonball — for use to attack or defend.

Amphibious: Of or relating to a military landing that combines land and naval forces.

Annexation: The incorporation or attachment of a territory into an existing political unit.

Artillery: Soldiers who specialize in the use of heavy weapons, such as cannon.

Barracks: A building or group of buildings used to house military personnel.

Battery: Placement of artillery (soldiers and weapons).

Brevet: A higher rank but not higher pay.

Brigade: A military combat unit commanded by a brigadier general or a colonel.

Cadet: A student at a military school training to become an officer.

Casualties: In war, the victims: the injured, killed, captured, or missing in action.

Cavalry: A division of the army that fights on horseback.

Commendation: An award for distinction in military operation.

Commission: An official government document that bestows powers and rank on someone in the military.

Confederacy: In the American Civil War, the alliance of states that broke ties with the U.S.

government to form a new government, called the Confederate States of America. The states that did not secede supported the Union.

Corps: In the military, a separate combat division with a special assignment.

Court-martial: A military trial that is held when a member of the military is accused of a crime.

Dyspepsia: Indigestion.

Engagement: In military terms, the meeting of enemy forces; a battle.

Entrench: To surround with a trench for defensive purposes.

Federal: Of, relating to, or loyal to the Union cause during the Civil War.

Flank: In a battle, the side of a formation of soldiers.

Fortification: The act or process of making a position strong or secure. Also, a military structure.

Furlough: Temporary leave from the army.

Garrison: A military post, often one that is permanently established. Also, the troops stationed at a post.

Hamlet: A small village.

Hardtack: A hard biscuit made of flour and water without salt.

Howitzer: A type of cannon.

Infantry: The branch of the military consisting of soldiers who are trained to fight on foot.

Provisional: Tentative or conditional.

Rebel: A person who opposes the authority in power. In the Civil War, "Rebel" became another word for Confederate.

Reconnaissance: An inspection of an area to gather military information.

Recruit: noun — a new member of an organization, often the military; verb — to persuade someone to join the military.

Regiment: A military unit of ground troops. *Regimental* refers to something orderly and strict.

Repulse: To drive or beat back.

Rural: Of, relating to, or associated with the country.

Sabbath: In this case, the first day of the week, Sunday, which is a day of rest and worship for many Christians.

Skirmish: A small conflict between enemies that can often lead to a larger battle.

Sorrel: A reddish-brown color.

Tithe: To give one-tenth of an income to a church.

Typhoid fever: A highly infectious disease that is transmitted by contaminated food or water.

Union: In the American Civil War, the states that supported the United States government. The states that did not support the U.S. seceded to form the Confederate States of America.

Verbatim: Word for word.

Index

Allegheny Mountains: 22
Appomattox Court House (Virginia): 27
Army of Northern Virginia: 22, 27, 28, 30, 33, 35
Ashby, Turner: 24
Barry, John: 35
Battles
    Antietam (Maryland): 22, 30, 35
    Chancellorsville (Virginia): 27, 31–37, 40, 42
    Fort Sumter (South Carolina): 20
    Fredericksburg (Virginia): 18, 30, 32, 35, 42
    Gettysburg (Pennsylvania): 22, 35
    Harpers Ferry (Virginia, now West Virginia): 39
    Manassas, First (Bull Run) (Virginia): 10, 20,
        21, 35, 42
    Manassas, Second (Bull Run) (Virginia): 26,
        27–30, 35
        Brawner Farm: 27
        Chinn Ridge: 30
        Groveton: 27, 28
        Henry Hill: 30
    Seven Days (Virginia): 30, 35
    Shenandoah Valley Campaign (Virginia):
        22–25, 27, 39
        Cross Keys: 23, 24
        Fort Royal: 24
        Kernstown: 23
        McDowell: 24
        Port Republic: 24
        Winchester: 24
    Wilderness Campaign (Virginia): 28, 32–35
Bee, Barnard E.: 10, 21
Blue Ridge Mountains: 22
Brake, Isaac: 5, 6
Bristoe Station (Virginia): 25
Centreville (Virginia): 27, 30
Clarksburg (Virginia): 4
Grant, Ulysses S.: 10, 27
Harrisburg (Pennsylvania): 22
Henry House Hill: 21
Hooker, Joseph: 32, 33, 35
Jackson, Cummins: 5, 6
Jackson, Elinor Junkin: 17, 18
Jackson, Elizabeth: 4
Jackson, Jonathan: 4
Jackson, Julia: 18, 31, 32, 36
Jackson, Julia Neale: 4, 5
Jackson, Laura: 4–6
Jackson, Mary Anna Morrison: 18, 31, 36, 39, 40
Jackson, Mary Graham: 18, 37
Jackson, Thomas J. (Stonewall):
    childhood: 4–6

    education: 6, 7–8
    gardening: 19
    life in Lexington: 16–19
    nicknames for: 17, 20, 21, 24
    religion: 11, 16, 19, 25, 36
    U.S.-Mexican War: 10–13
    Virginia Military Institute (VMI): 16–19
Jackson, Warren: 4–6
Jackson's Mill (Virginia): 5
King, Rufus: 27
Lee, Robert E.: 10, 27–30, 32, 33, 35, 36, 37
Lexington (Virginia): 11, 16, 18, 19, 37, 42
Lexington Presbyterian Church: 11, 19, 37
Little Sorrel: 35, 38–40
Longstreet, James: 27–30
Manassas Junction (Virginia): 20, 21, 26
McClellan, George B.: 23, 28
McDowell, Irvin: 21
Monterrey (Mexico): 10
Neale, Alfred: 6
New Orleans (Louisiana): 10
Paxton, E.F.: 42
Polk, James K.: 9
Pope, John: 26–30
Porter, Fitz John: 28–30
Potomac River: 22, 24
Rappahannock River: 32
Richmond (Virginia): 19, 20, 22, 23, 32, 36, 40
Scott, Winfield: 12
Shenandoah Valley (Virginia): 22–24
Slavery: 19
Stonewall Brigade: 21, 42
Stonewall Jackson Cemetery, Monument: 18, 37
Stuart, J.E.B.: 35
Taylor, Francis: 10–12
Taylor, Zachary: 10
Thoroughfare Gap (Virginia): 27, 28
U.S.-Mexican War: Battles in Cerro Gordo,
    Chapultepec, Churubusco, Contreras, Mexico
    City, Port Isabel, Veracruz: 9, 10, 11, 12, 13,
    17, 27, 28
U.S. Military Academy at West Point (New York):
    6–10, 17
Virginia Historical Society: 19
Virginia Military Institute (VMI):16–19, 37, 40, 41
Walker, James Alexander: 41, 42
Warrenton Turnpike (Virginia): 27
Washington College (Lexington): 17, 18
Washington, DC: 20, 21, 30
White, William: 11
Woodson, Blake B.: 5

COBBLESTONE®

The CIVIL WAR Series

F ew events in our nation's history have been as dramatic as those leading up to and during the Civil War. People held strong views on each side of the Mason-Dixon line, and the clash of North and South had far-reaching consequences for our country that are still being felt today.

Each 48-page book delivers the solidly researched content *COBBLESTONE*® is known for, written in an engaging manner that is sure to retain the attention of young readers. Perfect for report research or pursuing an emerging interest in the Civil War, these resources will complete your collection of materials on this important topic.

Each sturdy, hardcover volume includes:

- Fair and balanced depictions of people and events
- Well-researched text ■ Historical photographs
- Glossary ■ Time line

$17⁹⁵ each

NATION AT WAR: SOLDIERS, SAINTS, AND SPIES	**COB67900**
YOUNG HEROES OF THE NORTH AND SOUTH	**COB67901**
ABRAHAM LINCOLN: DEFENDER OF THE UNION	**COB67902**
GETTYSBURG: BOLD BATTLE IN THE NORTH	**COB67903**
ANTIETAM: DAY OF COURAGE AND SACRIFICE	**COB67904**
ROBERT E. LEE: DUTY AND HONOR	**COB67905**
ULYSSES S. GRANT: CONFIDENT LEADER AND HERO	**COB67906**
STONEWALL JACKSON: SPIRIT OF THE SOUTH	**COB67907**
JEFFERSON DAVIS AND THE CONFEDERACY	**COB67908**
REBUILDING A NATION: PICKING UP THE PIECES	**COB67909**

Buy 3 books and get our Time Line Poster FREE!

Our books are available through all major wholesalers, as well as directly from us.